GROWING IN THE GOSPEL

MODERNIZING JESUS' PARABLES

RETELLING THE PARABLES WITH MODERN DAY CULTURE AND COMMENTARY FROM THE OLD TESTAMENT

UPDATED

Michael Harvey Koplitz

The NASB uses italic to indicate words that have been added for clarification. Citations are shown with large capital letters.

Produced by Michael Harvey Koplitz

Table of Contents

Introduction

Jesus's parables can be viewed as summaries of haggadic midrash. Aggadic midrash is artistically written midrash (stories about biblical passages. Identifying the Aggadic midrash allows construction of modern parables using today's culture, helping Christians and non-Christians better understand Jesus' parables. Jesus constructed his parables using His culture; therefore, we can do the same thing.

The twist in the parable needs to be observed and maintained when the haggadic midrash is developed from the parable. The creation of parables from Aggadic midrash is storytelling that was used to help explain a biblical passage or something about God. They are learning tools used by rabbis to convey information, knowledge, and learning.

One could consider the parables a part of the advanced class of midrash training. Perhaps the use of parables was to ensure that the students of the rabbi are the only ones who understand the rabbi. In Jesus's day, a lot of His teaching would have done outdoors. Using parables could ensure someone overhearing, whether intentional, would not understand the lesson being offered. Persons not a part of the rabbi's circle would probably not question the rabbi about his parable because it was culturally wrong to do so.

The premise about parables being drawn from haggadic midrash is that the students of the rabbi would know not only the biblical stories but also the "main line" midrash about the biblical stories being discussed. Then the parable would make sense to them. Therefore, to truly understand a Jesus' parable, one needs to seek the biblical information from the

Hebrew Scriptures and the midrash He is using.[1]

[1] This concept is discovered in the book "Uncovering Mysteries of the Parables with Haggadic Midrash" by Dr. Anne Kimball Davis. This is a major research source in the parable discussions but not limited only to this source.

Biblical Proof of Semitic Bible Study Methods

It is vital to come to an understanding of what the original writers and the original listeners of the Christian Scriptures thought so that we can understand what God is telling us. The Bible is such a complex document, which is the Word of God and has an infinite number of messages it is convening to us. Since God is infinite, then certainly his Word is infinite. Using First century Bible studies techniques will help us learn what God was telling the people at the time the Scripture was written. Once we have a firm understanding of the original meaning, we can then expand our understanding of the Word and certainly can bring it into today's world.

Unfortunately, over the centuries the church left its Jewish roots behind and even denied its mother religion. The Christian Scriptures, which most persons call the New Testament, were written by Jews using their Hebraic understanding of God from the Hebrew Scripture and from the Midrash. As hermeneutics developed the understanding and study of the Scriptures, this science went in a different direction. Greek thought, which is used today by Seminaries, Universities and most preachers, look to analyze the Word of God in a sterile environment which comprises special rules, methods and regulations.

Those of us who attended seminary learned how to do hermeneutics. Unfortunately, we were also told the instructor was always correct, of course by the instructor. So, to pass the class, one had to regurgitate the instructor's analysis and belief when doing exegetical work. I am not saying my professors in seminary were wrong in their analysis; I am saying they did not open the different ways of studying the Scripture beyond the Greek hermeneutical way. It was not until I was out of Seminary that I learned about first century Bible study techniques.

Now it is time to explore the Scriptures to see if God promotes understanding the Christian Scriptures using the Hebraic Scriptures and Midrash. I start with the following Scriptures:

NIV **Acts 2:1** When the day of Pentecost came, they were all together in one place. 2
Suddenly a sound like the blowing of a violent wind came from heaven and filled the whole
house where they were sitting. 3 They saw what seemed to be tongues of fire that separated
and came to rest on each of them. 4 All of them were filled with the Holy Spirit and began
to speak in other tongues as the Spirit enabled them. 5 Now there were staying in Jerusalem
God-fearing Jews from every nation under heaven. 6 When they heard this sound, a crowd
came together in bewilderment, because each one heard their own language being spoken. 7
Utterly amazed, they asked: "Aren't all these who are speaking Galileans? 8 Then how is it
that each of us hears them in our native language? 9 Parthians, Medes and Elamites;
residents of Mesopotamia, Judea and Cappadocia, Pontus and Asia, 10 Phrygia and
Pamphylia, Egypt and the parts of Libya near Cyrene; visitors from Rome 11 (both Jews and
converts to Judaism); Cretans and Arabs-- we hear them declaring the wonders of God in
our own tongues!" 12 Amazed and perplexed, they asked one another, "What does this
mean?" 13 Some, however, made fun of them and said, "They have had too much wine." 14
Then Peter stood up with the Eleven, raised his voice and addressed the crowd: "Fellow
Jews and all of you who live in Jerusalem, let me explain this to you; listen carefully to what
I say. 15 These people are not drunk, as you suppose. It's only nine in the morning! 16 No,
this is what was spoken by the prophet Joel: 17 "'In the last days, God says, I will pour out
my Spirit on all people. Your sons and daughters will prophesy, your young men will see
visions, your old men will dream dreams. 18 Even on my servants, both men and women, I
will pour out my Spirit in those days, and they will prophesy. 19 I will show wonders in the
heavens above and signs on the earth below, blood and fire and billows of smoke. 20 The
sun will be turned to darkness and the moon to blood before the coming of the great and

glorious day of the Lord. [21] And everyone who calls on the name of the Lord will be saved.' (Acts 2:1-21 NIV)

The Bible describes the Pentecost saying after the Holy Spirit descended upon the Apostles and followers, they could speak in different tongues (languages) to the people who were around them. The power of the Holy Spirit enabled the followers of Jesus to tell all around them about the prophecy of what would happen.

[28] "And afterward, I will pour out my Spirit on all people. Your sons and daughters will prophesy, your old men will dream dreams, your young men will see visions. [29] Even on my servants, both men and women, I will pour out my Spirit in those days. (Joel 2:28-29 NIV)

Take note that there is a cause → effect relationship in the story. The Holy Spirit came upon the followers of Jesus who were together and gave them the power of prophecy by telling the people about the Messiah. When the people around the followers, who were not affected by the Holy Spirit, asked about what had happened, Peter rose in front of the crowd and did a Bible study for them. Peter explained what had just happened by using the Hebrew Scripture!

Therefore, just from this one story, we find that the Christian Scripture endorses using Hebraic Scripture to understand biblical passages.

This is the very beginning of this research. So, let us go on a journey to understand Jesus' parables using His culture and the Old Testament and write some modern day parables to help the readers of the Scripture today.

A Kingdom Divided Parable (Mark 3:23-29)

The Parables:

[22] And the teachers of the law who came down from Jerusalem said, "He is possessed by Beelzebul! By the prince of demons, he is driving out demons." (Mk. 3:22 NIV)

[23] So Jesus called them over to him and began to speak to them in parables: "How can
Satan drive out Satan? [24] If a kingdom is divided against itself, that kingdom cannot stand.
[25] If a house is divided against itself, that house cannot stand. [26] And if Satan opposes
himself and is divided, he cannot stand; his end has come. [27] In fact, no one can enter a
strong man's house without first tying him up. Then he can plunder the strong man's
house. [28] Truly I tell you, people can be forgiven all their sins and every slander they utter,
[29] but whoever blasphemes against the Holy Spirit will never be forgiven; they are guilty of
an eternal sin." (Mk. 3:23-29 NIV)

Modern Parable:

In the mid-1980's I worked for Flinchbaugh Products in Red Lion which was a division of the General Defense Corporation. In Red Lion practice, tank shells were manufactured for the United States Army so the tank solders could learn and practice firing shells at any enemy. During this time, President Ronald Regan determined that to prevent a war and the spread of the Evil Axis – the Soviet Union – the U.S. had to build up its military. Thus, to fight evil, which would use military might and possibly nuclear weapons, the U.S. had to adopt the method of evil and be prepared. Thus, to fight the potential invasion of evil and its use of war machines to kill people, the U.S. had to be prepared to fight back in the same way.

During World War II, the Nazis of Germany created a huge war machine and invaded many of Europe's countries. Their method was to drop bombs from airplanes and invade with troops and vehicles. They spread pure evil over Europe and Northern Africa, doing some horrible things. To fight the evil Satan placed upon their hearts, the Allies had to amass a huge army with the same munitions to destroy the evil. Thus, they used the methods of evil, the war machine, to defeat evil.

Commentary:
To fully understand this parable, we must understand what the Hebraic thoughts about Satan were. Satan is also referred to by his function which is "the accuser." This function is to tell the LORD about all the sins one commits (as if God does not know your sins already) and to demand justice. Satan desires to possess souls rejected from Heaven so he can build up his army. Satan can also be tricky convincing us to do what is wrong in the sight of the LORD while all the time we believe we are doing the right thing. Zechariah 3:1 explains to us that Satan stands beside the angel of the LORD to accuse us.

[NIV] **Zechariah 3:1** Then he showed me Joshua the high priest standing before the angel of the LORD, and Satan standing at his right side to accuse him. [2] The LORD said to Satan, "The LORD rebuke you, Satan! The LORD, who has chosen Jerusalem, rebuke you! Is not this man a burning stick snatched from the fire?" [3] Now Joshua was dressed in filthy clothes as he stood before the angel. [4] The angel said to those who were standing before him, "Take off his filthy clothes." Then he said to Joshua, "See, I have taken away your sin, and I will put fine garments on you." [5] Then I said, "Put a clean turban on his head." So, they put a clean turban on his head and clothed him, while the angel of the LORD stood by. [6] The angel of the LORD gave this charge to Joshua: [7] "This is what the LORD Almighty says: 'If you will walk in obedience to me and keep my requirements, then you will govern my house and have charge of my courts, and I will give you a place among these standing here.

A side note to this passage is Satan stands at the right side of the Angel of the Lord to accuse Joshua the High Priest of sinful activities. This may have led to the idea that Jesus will be at the right hand of the LORD, especially at the time of judgment. Therefore, instead of being accused by Satan, it will be Jesus who will protect us if we have confessed our sin and repented.

In 1 Chronicles 21 we find Satan revolted against Israel, God's people, to get souls. He did this by convincing King David to hold a census.

NIV **1 Chronicles 21:1** Satan rose up against Israel and incited David to take a census of Israel. 2 So David said to Joab and the commanders of the troops, "Go and count the Israelites from Beersheba to Dan. Then report back to me so that I may know how many there are." 3 But Joab replied, "May the LORD multiply his troops a hundred times over. My lord the king, are they not all my lord's subjects? Why does my lord want to do this? Why should he bring guilt on Israel?" 4 The king's word, however, overruled Joab; so, Joab left and went throughout Israel and then came back to Jerusalem. 5 Joab reported the number of the fighting men to David: In all Israel there were one million one hundred thousand men who could handle a sword, including four hundred and seventy thousand in Judah. 6 But Joab did not include Levi and Benjamin in the numbering, because the king's command was repulsive to him. 7 This command was also evil in the sight of God; so, he punished Israel. 8 Then David said to God, "I have sinned greatly by doing this. Now, I beg you, take away the guilt of your servant. I have done a very foolish thing."

Why is it sinful to take a census that God did not order? When David took the census, he was doing it for himself, saying to God that the people belonged to Him. God owns His people, including us. Therefore, only God can order a census to be taken. There is a penalty to take a consensus on your own, which is in Exodus 30:12.

12 "When you take a census of the Israelites to count them, each one must pay the LORD a ransom for his life at the time he is counted. Then no plague will come on them when you number them. (Exodus 30:12)

Satan can also try to deceive us by disguising himself as something beautiful. This belief can be seen in the following passage that became a part of the Talmud.

Rabbi Akiva used to scoff at sinners for giving in to their desires. One day, Satan appeared to him in the guise of a beautiful woman in a tree. Rabbi Akiva grabbed the tree and began climbing it, but when he reached halfway, Satan left him saying: Had they not declared in Heaven, "Beware of Rabbi Akiva and his Torah" your life would not have been worth two maahs[2]. (Kiddushin 81a).

Also in the following Talmud story:

> "One afternoon, before the Day of Atonement, Satan appeared to Plimo disguised as a poor man. He came to beg at Plimo's door and was brought some bread. He said: On a day like today when everyone is inside, should I be outside? He was brought into the house and given some bread. He said: On a day like today when everyone is eating at a table, should I be eating alone? They brought him in and sat him at the table. As he sat, he caused his body to be covered with boils and ulcers, and proceeded to behave in a most disgusting manner. Plimo told him to sit properly. He then asked for a cup of wine. When it was given to him, he coughed and spat his phlegm into the cup. They scolded him, so he pretended to die. Satan then caused Plimo to hear voices outside saying: Plimo killed someone. Plimo ran away and hid in an outhouse. Satan followed him there and Plimo [not realizing who it was] fell before him. When Satan saw how much Plimo was suffering, he revealed his identity. Satan then said to Plimo: Why do you say this prayer [i.e., an arrow in Satan's eyes]? What should I say, asked Plimo? Say: May the Merciful Lord rebuke Satan (Kiddushin 81a-81b).

[2] A type of currency

Satan can (and generally will) appear when you are about to do something righteous as shown in the following Midrash. Also, Satan will attempt to convince you that the righteous act you are about to do is not from God.

On the way to Isaac's sacrifice, Satan ran ahead of Abraham and appeared before him disguised as an old man. Satan asked Abraham where he was going. Abraham replied: To pray. Satan asked Abraham: "And does one who goes to pray have fire and a knife in his hand and wood on his shoulder?" Abraham replied: "We may tarry there a day or two, and we will have to slaughter [an animal for meat], bake bread, and eat." Satan said: "Old man, was I not there when God told you to take your son? And an old man like you is going to go and destroy a son that was given to him at the age of one hundred? Did you not hear the proverb: 'That which he had in his hand he destroyed and [now]seeks from others?'

[not part of the Midrash] Seeing his arguments were not working, Satan, the guise of the old man, tried another tactic, asking Abraham, in effect, how do you know that this commandment came to you from God?

You listen to the accuser [i.e., not God] and destroy a soul for which you will be judged guilty in court. Abraham said: I did not hear it from the accuser but from the blessed Lord; I will not listen to you.

[not in the midrash [Satan does not give up that easily. He left Abraham and went to work on Abraham's son, Isaac.

Satan then appeared as a young man and stood on the right side of Isaac. He asked Isaac where he and his father were going. Isaac replied: to study Torah. Satan asked: While you are alive or dead? Isaac said: Is there then a person who can learn after death? Satan said:

humiliated one [i.e., you are a doormat], son of a humiliated one, how many fasts did your mother fast until you were born. And that old man went crazy and he is going to slaughter you. Isaac replied: despite this, I will not violate the will of my creator or the command of my father (Midrash Tanchuma, Vayera 22)."

Now, with a strong understanding of Satan, let us move forward.

The divided Kingdom:

If a house is divided against itself, that house cannot stand. (Mark 3:25)

Imagery from this event is being invoked here. The 12 tribes of Israel were once a single Kingdom under the rule of Saul, David, and Solomon. When the 10 northern tribes broke away, they divided the kingdom into two parts. In the north, they worshiped Adonai יְהֺוָה by placing two golden calves at the north and south of the divided northern kingdom:

TNK **2 Chronicles 13:8** Now you are bent on opposing the kingdom of the LORD, which is in the charge of the sons of David, because you are a great multitude and possess the golden calves that Jeroboam made for you as gods. (2 Chr. 13:8 TNK)

While in the Southern kingdom Adonai was worshiped at the Temple in Jerusalem. In the North Adonai sat on the throne created by the two golden calves while in the South Adonai sat on the throne created by the Ark of the Covenant. The Northern Kingdom was destroyed according to the Southern Kingdom because they divided from the South and practiced a unique way of worshiping God. A house divided by itself cannot survive. Thus, the loss of the 10 tribes to the Assyrian and the almost destruction of the South.

The "Strong Man" imagery would bring up the vision of the time of Moses. The vision of Moses going into the House of Pharaoh, the Strong Man, and having to tie him up before Moses could take Israel from Egypt. The LORD gave Moses the plagues to tie up Pharaoh. When the ten plagues hit Egypt, the people of Egypt cried out to their Pharaoh to stop the punishment. The only way for the plagues to stop was to allow his house to be plundered by letting Moses take Israel. If the LORD wants a house of a strong man to be robbed, he will give you the ability to do so.

So, Jesus was given the ability to break into Satan's house, the Strong Man, so that He can free us from slavery. Jesus was not Satan but had to use some of Satan's techniques to defeat Him. The Zohar tells us there are times righteous people need to use the techniques of those who are under the influence of the Evil Inclination for righteousness to prevail, for example: Rachel who stole her father's (Laban's) idols. She did this to help her father to realize that the idols were not God. She had to commit theft, a crime, to solve a crime, idolatry.

So, with the understanding of Satan the Accuser and the Strong Man imagery, it is clear what is happening in this parable. Jesus commanded the evil spirits in people to leave them, which is something Satan can do to free the people from the evil spirit. By doing this, Jesus could be seen by his contemporaries as being Satan in disguise. He was NOT Satan in disguise. He was using Satan's ways against him.

Certainly, Satan could send an angel or himself to undo his work. Why would he undo his work? A house divided cannot stand by itself is the symbolism that one would not build a house just to tear it down, so Satan would not possess people just to let them go. So, the bottom line is the people needed to understand that Jesus was doing God's work by standing up to Satan and beating him at his own game.

Parable of the Net (Matthew 13:47-50)

The Parable:

[47] "Once again, the kingdom of heaven is like a net that was let down into the lake and caught all kinds of fish. [48] When it was full, the fishermen pulled it up on the shore. Then they sat down and collected the good fish in baskets, but threw the bad away. [49] This is how it will be at the end of the age. The angels will come and separate the wicked from the righteous [50] and throw them into the blazing furnace, where there will be weeping and gnashing of teeth. (Mat 13:47-50 NIV)

The Modern Parable:

One day, a new pastor came to his new church appointment (church). The pastor wanted to discover what the emphasis of the church was. He knew it was essential to learn about the people and what drove them. So, the new pastor got a calendar of events for the year from the church secretary.

What he discovered was that 95% of the church activities revolved around the congregation. There were the usual Sunday worship celebrations and Sunday school events. The choir rehearsed every week except for June, July, and August. There were a lot of various committees which meet monthly. There were even a few fellowship events during the year.

The pastor saw there were a couple of fund-raising events on the calendar. The pastor started seeking outreach, mission, and community events. Did the church interact with the neighborhood in which it lived? He found a couple of events that were clearly developed to bring the Gospel of Christ to the community.

When the pastor examined the church budget, only 1% was dedicated for outreach projects. The church had a 20% budget to give money to Christian organizations that outreached into the community. About 95% of the congregation was proud to have given 20% of their budget to missions. These people did not want to be hands on with any mission project. Instead, they gave money to others to do hands-on work.

The 5% who did all they could to bring the Gospel of Jesus Christ to the community spoke to the pastor about this situation. The pastor tried to get the rest of the congregation to understand that giving money is great, but they are the hands and feet of Jesus. After 2 years, the pastor decided no matter what he said, no matter how many biblical references he offered, the 95% would not move forward. So, one day, he asked his congregation what the definition is of being a disciple of Jesus Christ. The answer he received did not surprise him because it matched up to the church's calendar.

One Sunday at worship, Jesus appeared at the rear of the church. There was amazement and fear as Jesus read off the names of the people who were coming with him to heaven. It was the 5% who spent their time and resources trying to spread the Gospel, the hands-on people. Jesus also took the pastor with him.

The rest of the congregation immediately broke into weeping and gnashing of teeth. Why were they left behind? They never understood why they were left behind.

Commentary:

Why do people come to church? There are many reasons however, we can look at a few compelling reasons. There are people who attend church because they feel compelled because of their upbringing. Mom and Dad always went to church on Sunday, therefore, they must go to church. They see church as one hour, maybe two hours if they attend Sunday school, and they give some money to doing Christ's work. Over the last fifty years, professional mission and outreach organizations have appeared in our culture, thus taking the hands-on work away from our church people. So, today you can feel good about helping those who are in need without ever seeing or meeting them. This spills over into the attendance at the church. What this means is there are church congregations who refuse to accept people who differ from they are. Oh yes, they have one or two people that are ethnically different. But that is it.

God is from Missouri – meaning God is going to know your heart based on your actions. Belief is expressed actions? So, if you say you want to share the Gospel of Jesus Christ with everyone in the world but you refuse to do any hands-on work, let us say, with poor people and you do not want the poor people in your church then you are showing God you do not want the Gospel spread to all people. Saying Jesus is for everyone but not at this church is not acceptable.

Unfortunately, many people in our churches think they are good disciples by attending church once a week and giving some money to the church and some causes. The original parable tells us that Jesus knows who are the good and the bad people. Jesus knows who is putting up a façade and who the real disciples are.

There are several parables that are on this topic, which clarifies that Jesus is telling us to STOP worrying about those people. Do the work of the Gospel and stop caring about the other people! Jesus will separate the true disciples from the façade disciples. That's Jesus' job and not ours.

As Saint Paul said, do not let these facade disciples be a stumbling block. If they become a stumbling block to your true discipleship, then it is time to find a different worshiping community. Remember, every congregation will have those people who want the inexpensive discipleship (cheap grace).

Parable of the tenants (Matthew 21:37-44)

The Parable:

33 "Listen to another parable: There was a landowner who planted a vineyard. He put a wall around it, dug a winepress in it and built a watchtower. Then he rented the vineyard to some farmers and moved to another place. 34 When the harvest time approached, he sent his servants to the tenants to collect his fruit. 35 "The tenants seized his servants; they beat one, killed another, and stoned a third. 36 Then he sent other servants to them, more than the first time, and the tenants treated them the same way. 37 Last of all, he sent his son to them. 'They will respect my son,' he said. 38 "But when the tenants saw the son, they said to each other, 'This is the heir. Come, let's kill him and take his inheritance.' 39 So they took him and threw him out of the vineyard and killed him. 40 "Therefore, when the owner of the vineyard comes, what will he do to those tenants?" 41 "He will bring those wretches to a wretched end," they replied, "and he will rent the vineyard to other tenants, who will give him his share of the crop at harvest time." 42 Jesus said to them, "Have you never read in the Scriptures: ""The stone the builders rejected has become the cornerstone; the Lord has done this, and it is marvelous in our eyes'? 43 "Therefore I tell you that the kingdom of God will be taken away from you and given to a people who will produce its fruit 44 Anyone who falls on this stone will be broken to pieces; anyone on whom it falls will be crushed." (Mat 21:33-44 NIV)

The Modern Parable:

There once was a young couple who decided that they wanted to buy a house and start a family. So, they went and found a real estate agent and went looking for a house. Unfortunately, they did not have enough money for the down payment, so the only option left to them was a rent to own a house. For several weeks, they went and looked at various houses until he found one that appealed to them. They entered a contract for the rent to own home, signed the contract, and moved in.

After a few years, the couple decided they liked the house. however, they did not like paying the monthly rent, so they stop paying the rent. They received a letter from the owner asking why they were not paying the rent. The couple ignored the letter and continued living in the house. A certified letter, then a registered letter, and eventually phone calls about why the couple was not paying the rent. The owner tried to be fair to the couple, giving them every opportunity to pay the rent that they owed him.

After a time, the owner decided he had to evict the couple and get back his property, but by now the couple had two small children and he felt guilty about kicking them out into the cold. So, the owner decided not to do anything about it and allowed the couple and their children to stay there if they wanted to rent free.

Several friends of the owner said to him he had every right to kick the family out of his house and that he should get a lawyer and do that. The owner replied he knew he could do this, but he did not want to because he had compassion for the family and hoped in time that they would do the right thing. After all, the family was taking diligent care of the house, they just were not paying the rent.

Commentary:

The pure Christian interpretation of this parable is Jesus is condemning the Jewish leadership for not accepting Him as the true Messiah and therefore the true leader of the Jewish religion. Perhaps that is exactly what Jesus is doing. However, there is another side to this parable that is worth exploring. When Adonai brought the children of Israel out of Egypt, he led them to Mount Sinai where they entered a treaty with him, which we call the

Ten Commandments. The treaty is quite simple, and it states that Adonai is the greater power and that he would take care of the lesser power Israel, as long as they followed his laws and regulations. The expansion of the Ten Commandments is what we call the Torah, or the first five books of the Bible.

When we examine Israel's history as presented to us in the Hebrew Scriptures, we can see that Israel violated the treaty with Adonai frequently. The writers of the history interpreted the doom and gloom that came to Israel as a punishment from God but it was not a punishment, rather God took away his protection, that is he stopped taking care of them, allowing the enemies of Israel to overrun the country and eventually the destruction of the ten northern tribes and the Babylonian exile.

An excellent example of the cycle of following the Sinai treaty with Adonai, breaking the treaty, reestablishing the treaty can be seen in the book of Judges. There are twelve stories contained within telling us about this exact pattern. In each of these patterns and throughout history, Adonai has always offered forgiveness to Israel for violating the Sinai treaty.

This parable was discussing this cycle of Israel violating the treaty with Adonai and then Adonai forgiving them. What Jesus was offering the people of Israel in his day was a new treaty with the people that did not supersede the Sinai treaty but enhanced the treaty, allowing for violations of it and for God's forgiveness when it happened. It is this concept of an enhanced covenant that the religious leadership of Israel was objecting to. This enhanced covenant would be established on the day of the crucifixion and reinforced upon the resurrection of Jesus. So, the religious leadership of Israel was not rejecting Jesus, but they were objecting to an enhanced covenant which would take away much of their power allowing forgiveness to occur through Jesus' sacrifice on the cross.

In the modern parable, you can see how a treaty was established between the couple and the owner of the house. The couple decided they did not want to pay the rent anymore, but instead of kicking them out immediately, the owner tried to get them to live up to their part of the treaty. Over time, the owner decided he wanted to set a new treaty in place so that if the couple took care of the house, he would allow them to stay there rent free. Of course, the owner still kept ownership of the house and forgave them for not paying the rent. He established an enhanced treaty with them.

The Workers in the Vineyard (Matthew 20:1-16)

The Parable:

NIV **Matthew 20:1** "For the kingdom of heaven is like a landowner who went out early in
the morning to hire workers for his vineyard. [2] He agreed to pay them a denarius for the
day and sent them into his vineyard. [3] "About nine in the morning he went out and saw
others standing in the marketplace doing nothing. [4] He told them, 'You also go and work in
my vineyard, and I will pay you whatever is right.' [5] So they went. "He went out again about
noon and about three in the afternoon and did the same thing. [6] About five in the
afternoon he went oand found still others standing around. He asked them, 'Why have you
been standing here all day long doing nothing?' [7] "'Because no one has hired us,' they
answered. "He said to them, 'You also go and work in my vineyard.' [8] "When evening
came, the owner of the vineyard said to his foreman, 'Call the workers and pay them their
wages, beginning with the last ones hired and going on to the first.' [9] "The workers who
were hired about five in the afternoon came and each received a denarius. [10] So, when
those came who were hired first, they expected to receive more. But each one of them also
received a denarius. [11] When they received it, they began to grumble against the landowner.
[12] 'These who were hired last worked only one hour,' they said, 'and you have made them
equal to us who have borne the burden of the work and the heat of the day.' [13] "But he
answered one of them, 'I am not being unfair to you, friend. Did not you agree to work for
a denarius? [14] Take your pay and go. I want to give the one who was hired last the same as I
gave you. [15] Do not I have the right to do what I want with my own money? Or are you
envious because I am generous?'[16] "So the last will be first, and the first will be last."

The Modern Parable:

There was a small construction company who was looking to build single-family houses. One day, a young couple came into the office and ordered a large house. The contracts were signed, and the designs were approved. The builder was excited the next day to start work. But he needed laborers to help him. So, he went to the unemployment office around 7:00 AM and asked several men if they wanted to work. Unofficially, of course, the daily rate is $100. Several men agreed to work, so they were driven over to the site, and they started working. Then about 11:00 AM, the builder decided that the work would go faster if he got more laborers. So, back to the unemployment office to get more. Then at 3:00 PM he got some more workers.

At 5:00 PM, the work for the day was. The builder paid each worker, in cash, for the day's work. Each worker, no matter what time they started on the day, was paid $100. The workers who started at 7:00 AM were angry. Why did the workers who followed them get paid the same amount as they received? That was just not fair.

The builder looked at the men and said that it was his business, and each man got the amount of money agreed to $100 for the day. If they did not like the arrangement, then he would not hire them tomorrow. It was the builder's decision on how to reward the men for their work.

Commentary:

This parable talks about hiring workers in the marketplace. Consider this parable being based on the Adam and Eve story. The workers in the field are Adam's children. Seth Was the first of the workers for the vineyard. According to the Book of Adam and Eve, they had over three children. There would be plenty of workers for the fields. Of course, the children would be born in later years. In this analysis, the hours of the day correspond to the years the children were being born.

The souls of the children waiting to be born are in heaven and would be "standing here all day doing nothing." At the proper time, each soul would be born on Earth.

The vineyard is used in the Hebrew Scriptures as a symbol of Israel. The landowner is God, who attends to the needs of Israel. Why would God need to hire workers for his vineyard? The thought of needing workers is an echo found in the Hebrew Scriptures. So, this parable could be a Midrash about estate inheritance. First, the echo for the need for workers for the vineyard is shown in Genesis.

Gen. 2:18 The LORD God said, "It is not good for the man to be alone. I will make a helper suitable for him."

Gen. 2:20 But for Adam no suitable helper was found. [21] So the LORD God caused the man to fall into a deep sleep; and while he was sleeping, he took one of the man's ribs and then closed up the place with flesh. [22] Then the LORD God made a woman from the rib he had taken out of the man, and he brought her to the man. (Gen. 2:20-22 NIV)

[17] To Adam he said, "Because you listened to your wife and ate fruit from the tree about which I commanded you, 'You must not eat from it,' "Cursed is the ground because of you; through painful toil you will eat food from it all the days of your life. [18] It will produce thorns and thistles for you, and you will eat the plants of the field. [19] By the sweat of your brow you will eat your food until you return to the ground, since from it you were taken; for dust you are and to dust you will return." (Gen. 3:17-19 NIV)

Adam was placed in charge of Earth. Adam needed helpers to till the soil and plant gardens. So, as each child was born to Adam and Eve, when they were old enough, they would be sent out to the fields and would work. When time transpired, and Adam died the fields Adam cultivated (owned) was divided among his children. It would not matter how long each child had worked the field. The 5 o'clock workers could equate to those who just became old enough to work the field. Even a male infant would receive an equal portion of the inheritance from Adam.

Would it be fair in Jesus' day for an estate to be equally portioned out, except for the first-born who received more than the others? Even if a child left the farm and never worked, would it be fair for them to have a share in the estate? Valid questions. In today's world, the parents' estate may not be divided equally among the children. Could this have been done in Jesus' day? Deuteronomy 21 has the rules of inheritance.

If a man had two sons and the firstborn was born to the wife, he did not love, that child would still receive the double portion because he was the firstborn (Deuteronomy 21 – assuming he had two wives). Rebellious children were not tolerated as shown in Deuteronomy 21, so mostly children obeyed the parents and would work the field. So, we can put aside whether all the children would receive an inheritance.

As more children were born into the family, the portion of the inheritance would decrease for the other children, even the first-born. Could the parable be showing that the older children who worked the fields for a longer period must not be jealous of the children born later?

Using the family inheritance metaphor for this parable works to show how God's grace works. It does not matter when one comes to know God through Christ, each will receive an equal portion of God's grace – becoming a child of God. Of course, God's grace is infinite. Care must be taken to prevent the listener/reader from getting hung up on the limitation of the size of the estate.

Jesus is trying to explain to us the ways of the Kingdom of God in human terms.

Parable of the Lost Sheep (Matthew 18:12-13)

The Parable:

12 "What do you think? If a man owns a hundred sheep, and one of them wanders away,
will he not leave the ninety-nine on the hills and go to look for the one that wandered off?
13 And if he finds it, truly I tell you, he is happier about that one sheep than about the
ninety-nine that did not wander off. (Mat 18:12-13 NIV)

4 "Suppose one of you has a hundred sheep and loses one of them. Does not he leave the
ninety-nine in the open country and go after the lost sheep until he finds it? 5 And when he
finds it, he joyfully puts it on his shoulders 6 and goes home. Then he calls his friends and
neighbors together and says, 'Rejoice with me; I have found my lost sheep.' (Luk 15:4-6 NIV)

The Modern Parable:

The shepherd selected from the masses of sheep 100 sheep to call his own. He treated these sheep as family, giving them the best of whatever they needed and gave them things they wanted. Over the years, the sheep followed the voice of the shepherd. A relationship of trust developed between the shepherd and the sheep so that the sheep instinctively followed the instructions of the shepherd, whether or not the shepherd was with the sheep.

The shepherd took a vacation for a time, feeling assured the sheep would continue to follow his instructions. During the time the shepherd was not present, 99 of the sheep strayed away from the shepherd's instructions. The 99-sheep developed new instructions on living and convinced themselves that their interpretation of the shepherd's original instructions was correct.

One sheep was convinced that the 99 sheep were wrong. What was this sheep to do? The 1 sheep made himself lost. This 1 sheep strayed away from the 99 and followed the shepherd's original instructions. The 99-sheep pushed out this 1 sheep so that it was not a part of the flock anymore. So, the 1 sheep became lost. He was not a part of the flock because if the 99-other sheep allowed the 1 sheep to stay, he could corrupt others in the flock.

One day, the shepherd returned to see how well the flock was doing. He counted the sheep to discover that one was missing. He was also quite surprised that the 99 sheep had changed their ways of living and attending to each other from what the shepherd taught them. When the shepherd asked the 99 sheep about what happened to the 1 sheep, they told him that the 1 sheep did not want to be a part of the flock because he felt that the 99 sheep were not following what the shepherd had taught them.

The shepherd immediately left the flock and went in search of the lost sheep. Over time, the shepherd found the lost sheep and created a new flock, with this one sheep becoming the leader.

Commentary:

The 99 sheep in Jesus's parable and in the Midrash are the Pharisees and Sadducees who lived in Jesus' day. These groups of persons interpreted the Word of God the way they wanted to and not necessarily for the benefit of the people, but to fill their pockets with gold, silver, and power. God is the shepherd who created the flock and instructed the flock, the people, in His Word so that they would know what was expected of them and how God expected them to live. God is obviously the shepherd.

So, the 1 sheep who was made lost was a loyal disciple to Yahweh. Therefore, when God returns, He will separate people into two larger groups: those who interpreted and changed the Torah, and those who followed the Torah the best way they could, according to God.

Seven Times Parable (Matthew 18:21-35)

The Parable:

[21] Then Peter came to Jesus and asked, "Lord, how many times shall I forgive my brother
or sister who sins against me? Up to seven times?" [22] Jesus answered, "I tell you, not seven
times, but seventy-seven times. [23] "Therefore, the kingdom of heaven is like a king who
wanted to settle accounts with his servants. [24] As he began the settlement, a man who owed
him ten thousand bags of gold was brought to him. [25] Since he was not able to pay, the
master ordered that he and his wife and his children and all that he had be sold to repay the
debt. [26] "At this the servant fell on his knees before him. 'Be patient with me,' he begged,
'and I will pay back everything.' [27] The servant's master took pity on him, canceled the debt
and let him go. [28] "But when that servant went out, he found one of his fellow servants
who owed him a hundred silver coins. He grabbed him and began to choke him. 'Pay back
what you owe me!' he demanded. [29] "His fellow servant fell to his knees and begged him,
'Be patient with me, and I will pay it back.' [30] "But he refused. Instead, he went off and had
the man thrown into prison until he could pay the debt. [31] When the other servants saw
what had happened, they were outraged and went and told their master everything that had
happened. [32] "Then the master called the servant in. 'You wicked servant,' he said, 'I
canceled all that debt of yours because you begged me to. [33] Shouldn't you have had mercy
on your fellow servant just as I had on you?' [34] In anger his master handed him over to the
jailers to be tortured, until he should pay back all he owed. [35] "This is how my heavenly
Father will treat each of you unless you forgive your brother or sister from your heart."
(Mat 18:21-35 NIV)

The Modern Parable:

There was a college in which the faculty wanted the students to learn about collaboration and consensus. They believed by teaching collaboration and consensus, the students would learn about being in community. So, every freshman had to take a research class. The class was divided into groups of five and given a research assignment. What happened in the group was a leader was chosen. The leader created assignments for each person of the group to accomplish. So, off they went to do their research.

They came together one week later and discussed their discoveries. Four of the five students were ready and when the leader called upon them, the group saw the work they were doing. What about student number 5? He did nothing. He engaged in several rage parties during the week and just never got around to it. What is the problem student 5 wondered? So, what if he did not get the research done? There were two weeks left to submit the project. Student 5 assured the group he would do his work and off they went.

A week later, the same situation occurred. Student 5 did not do any work. What was the group to do? If they turned in the project, missing his material, they would not receive a passing grade. So, the leader of the group went to the instructor to discuss the situation. The leader complained heavily about student 5 not doing his part of the task. The leader told the instructor that the morale of the group was low, and they felt betrayed.

The instructor told the group leader she had to get the project done, even if student 5 does not do any of his assigned work. She was reminded that the group's grade was determined by the results turned in by the process. So, the leader called the group together without student 5 and told them what was going to happen. Each of them would collect a part of student 5's work and they would get it done. Wow, the complaining began. The group wanted to toss student 5 out of the group and make it clear to the class instructor that student 5 gets no credit for their work.

After a lengthy discussion, they got the work done without student 5's contribution but also to turn in the project with all five names on the project, thus preserving the group. So, a week later that is exactly what they did. They received an "A" on the project and all 5 students shared in the grade.

Commentary:

Chapter 18 of Matthew's Gospel is filled with a lot of parables about forgiveness. There is more to the parables than just forgiveness. Nearly all commentaries on this parable focus only on forgiveness. Forgiveness is in the parable, but I think the parable says a lot more.

The parable is discussing being in the community. How do we live together in harmony in a community? When you contemplate what Jesus' original listeners were thinking about, it must lead to community. If the people could not live together in harmony, they would destroy themselves and would not have to be concerned about the Romans. They needed to work together to survive.

Community life is a major feature of Jewish and early Christian life. To keep a community working together, forgiveness must be a key solution to problems. There will always be people in a community (or a small group) who will take advantage of the members of the community. In the modern parable, student 5 took the risk and did nothing to contribute to the assignment the group was given. Since the class was about collaboration and consensus, the instructor reminded the group leader that it was not acceptable to turn in the project, ignoring student 5.

Is it fair that student 5 got full credit for a project which he did not contribute? No, it is not fair. But it is reality. Lazy people will always exist in any community. If you concentrate on the lazy person, then the energy of the community will be redirected from the task and the community can fall apart. You have two choices: (1) offer forgiveness to the individual who is not holding up their end; (2) remove the person from the community.

If you remove a person from the community, another person will move into the void created and it is possible that the new person or another member of the community can decide to become lazy. Perhaps when student 5 was forgiven by the other students and he received an "A" on his report card, his heart might be changed.

A note about the original parable that fits this new way of examining the parable is from the last verse. If you do not forgive, then God will not forgive. Think about it as if you do not forgive, then the community will fall apart, and you will be "out in the cold." Community is the key to the parable. Maintaining our community!

Forgiveness can change our heart and the heart of the person receiving forgiveness. True forgiveness is life changing for all parties in the situation.

The Barren Fig Tree Parable (Luke 13:6-9)

The Parable:

[6] Then he told this parable: "A man had a fig tree growing in his vineyard, and he went to look for fruit on it but did not find any. [7] So he said to the man who took care of the vineyard, 'For three years now I've been coming to look for fruit on this fig tree and haven't found any. Cut it down! Why should it use up the soil?' [8] "'Sir,' the man replied, 'leave it alone for one more year, and I'll dig around it and fertilize it. [9] If it bears fruit next year, fine! If not, then cut it down.'" (Lk. 13:6-9 NIV)

The Modern Parable:

I loved my new home and wanted to beautify the land it was sitting on. So, I got up one morning and purchased a large number of arborvitae trees for the entire perimeter of the property except for the street edge. They were magnificent. I watered them every day and pruned them as necessary. The first year they grew well. But, the next year some of the arborvitae grew like weeds while any other withered and died. Many of the trees grew over six feet tall. One day I decided to pull them all out. But then I realized that the ones that did grow deserved the right to keep growing. So, I replaced the withered ones and tried to nurse them so that they would grow large like the other ones.

Commentary:

This parable uses an echo from the Old Testament dealing with the planting of trees and the bearing of fruit.

> [23] "'When you enter the land and plant any kind of fruit tree, regard its fruit as forbidden. For three years you are to consider it forbidden; it must not be eaten. [24] In the fourth year

all its fruit will be holy, an offering of praise to the LORD. [25] But in the fifth year you may eat its fruit. In this way your harvest will be increased. I am the LORD your God. (Lev. 19:23-25 NIV)

When a fruit tree is planted, any fruit that it produces cannot be eaten. Then, the fourth year, the fruit is offered to the Lord as an offering. So, after planting a fruit tree, one cannot enjoy the fruit from the tree until it has been planted for five years. In the parable, the tree has produced no fruit during its first three years. So, is the tree still under the Law? The owner of the tree agrees to let the tree live for another year to see if the fruit grows. A question would be if the tree produces fruit in the fourth year, does the owner have to wait another four years – three years to grow fruit and one year for the Lord as an offering? If so, the owner would have to wait eight years to enjoy the fruit.

"Over vigorous trees expend all their energy in growing wood and do not produce flower buds. Typically, this occurs for two reasons: over-fertilization and over-pruning. Heavy applications of nitrogen will stimulate excessive growth at the expense of flower production."[3]

Why do fruit trees grow and not bear fruit? The caretaker fertilizing the tree may just be continuing the effect of too much nitrogen for the tree. The tree might continue to grow and not produce any fruit. The best thing would not fertilize the tree or the surround ground.

"You say you do not fertilize the trees? But do you fertilize the lawn surrounding the trees? Fruit trees do not know that you are applying nitrogen only for the grass. Rain can move the nitrogen down past the grass roots where the trees can take it up. The solution—do

---

[3] http://extension.psu.edu/plants/gardening/fact-sheets/home-orchard-production/why-is-there-no-fruit-on-my-tree

not apply extra fertilizer to the lawn within 5 feet of the spread of the tree's branches. Be careful, because under fertilization can also occur."[4]

Is it possible God has "over fertilized" Israel? Looking at her history, it is debatable. Since the nation was destroyed and the people were under Roman control, the answer would be no. Their King was not Jewish and was not following the purity of the Torah laws. Gentiles were in the land bringing their pagan ways, which made the land unclean.

So, would the people of Judea and the Galilee be able to produce fruit for God under these circumstances? Is Jesus's parable telling us the people should have been bearing fruit for God even in those conditions? To answer the question affirmatively means to change the focus from a materialistic answer to a spiritual answer. Even under Roman and Herod rule, the people could continue growing in their spirituality. Then the parable takes a different twist.

The corruption of the religious leadership and the corruption of the Torah were what Jesus was referring to. The people's spiritual life was failing because of the desire for leadership to conform to Roman rule so they could keep their power positions.

A message to us today is to attend to our spiritual life as much, if not more than, our physical life. People who do not offer their tithe to God, do not attend God's worship, and never read their Bible are allowing their spiritual life to decay. They will not bear fruit for the Lord. How long do they believe Jesus will wait for them to realize the problem? The parable is a wake-up call to all people that their spiritual life is important and must not be neglected.

---

[4] IBID

The Parable of Lazarus and the Rich Man (Luke 16:19-31)

The Parable:

[19] "There was a rich man who was dressed in purple and fine linen and lived in luxury every day. [20] At his gate was laid a beggar named Lazarus, covered with sores [21] and longing to eat what fell from the rich man's table. Even the dogs came and licked his sores. [22] "The time came when the beggar died and the angels carried him to Abraham's side. The rich man also died and was buried. [23] In Hades, where he was in torment, he looked up and saw Abraham far away, with Lazarus by his side. [24] So he called to him, 'Father Abraham, have pity on me and send Lazarus to dip the tip of his finger in water and cool my tongue, because I am in agony in this fire.' [25] "But Abraham replied, 'Son, remember that in your lifetime you received your good things, while Lazarus received bad things, but now he is comforted here and you are in agony. [26] And besides all this, between us and you a great chasm has been set in place, so that those who want to go from here to you cannot, nor can anyone cross over from there to us.' [27] "He answered, 'Then I beg you, father, send Lazarus to my family, [28] for I have five brothers. Let him warn them, so that they will not also come to this place of torment.' [29] "Abraham replied, 'They have Moses and the Prophets; let them listen to them.' [30] "'No, father Abraham,' he said, 'but if someone from the dead goes to them, they will repent.' [31] "He said to him, 'If they do not listen to Moses and the Prophets, they will not be convinced even if someone rises from the dead.'" (Luk 16:19-31 NIV)

The Modern Parable:

The first day of class had arrived at the college. I was excited about the class I signed up for on creative writing. I wondered how the subject would be presented and especially how creativity was to be graded. The professor came into the room and welcomed us to the class. Then he distributed the syllabus for the class. He then told us how he wanted us to use our imagination. Therefore, he instituted a different, rather creative grading system.

He told us everyone in the class at that moment had an "A+" grade. Since he wanted us to be as creative as possible and not to worry about grading, he developed this odd method. So, all I had to do was to follow the rules of the class, and I would maintain my A+. The rules were quite simple: participate in class (which also meant showing up to class), and writing three creative papers on a subject to be given to us later.

This seemed simple to me, and I received my A+. I was surprised by the number of students in the class who did not come to class much and several who neglected to turn in the papers. Over 50% of the class did not receive the A+ while 30% failed the class.

The Kingdom of God is like this class. We all start with a perfect A+ grade. All we must do is follow the rules given to us in God's Word and we enter Heaven. Yet there are so many people who will not enter heaven.

Commentary:

The rich man refused to offer any charity to Lazarus in the story which is a requirement from God. The twist to the story is that Lazarus with sores on his body would not have been allowed inside of the community. People with skin diseases were always displaced. Here the rich man could have helped Lazarus, and the cost would have been minor. God gave this rich man resources for himself but also to help others. The rich man missed that point.

The Kingdom of God is open to all who come to believe in Jesus as Lord and Savior. Our entrance into Heaven is dependent on our behavior in this lifetime. So, we are starting by receiving an A+, the guarantee of perfection so we can enter Heaven.

Then it is up to us whether we are going to maintain our A+. The Bible has been given to us to assist us in maintaining the A+. We disintegrate our A+ by violating God's Word. We do not need to have warnings placed before us as we travel the road of life because we know upfront what the situation is. The students in the class maintained their A+ if they followed four simple rules. We maintain our A+ and entry into Heaven by following God's Word.

The Parable of the First and the Last (Luke 14:7-11)

The Parable:

[7] When he noticed how the guests picked the places of honor at the table, he told them this parable: [8] "When someone invites you to a wedding feast, do not take the place of honor, for a person more distinguished than you may have been invited. [9] If so, the host who invited both of you will come and say to you, 'Give this person your seat.' Then, humiliated, you will have to take the least important place. [10] But when you are invited, take the lowest place, so that when your host comes, he will say to you, 'Friend, move up to a better place.' Then you will be honored in the presence of all the other guests. [11] For all those who exalt themselves will be humbled, and those who humble themselves will be exalted." (Luk 14:7-11 NIV)

The Modern Parable:

There were two brothers, John and Jim, who were elated when it was announced that a baseball team, a minor league team, was moving to their city. A stadium was built for the team and when the first season was announced, both brothers became season ticket holders. They attended every home game and, when possible, some of the away games. They were great fans of the team.

After 6 six years, it was announced that the 1,000,000th fan through the front gate would receive an undisclosed grand prize. The brothers wondered what the prize could be. John determined right then that he would be that 1,000,000th fan and would win the prize. The season went on as usual until at one game it was announced at the next game the 1,000,000th fan would enter through the front gate.

John looked at the local paper that morning and the local sportswriter believed the first fan at the front gate would be the winner. The sportswriter added up the official game fan attendance and determined this outcome. John became even more determined to be that fan.

It was a rough day for John. Nothing went right that day for John. He was forced to leave later than he wanted to go to be first at the gate. Of course, the traffic was heavier than normal. But that did not stop John. He violated several traffic laws to get to the parking lot as quickly as possible. Now at the same time, Jim was having a normal day and when the time came to go to the ball game, he got into his car and drove off. He did not let the heavy traffic bother him. He even allowed several cars to come out of parking lots along the way. He was a courteous driver and even though he would like to have been the 1,000,000th fan; he remembered his childhood teachings of kindness to all.

John ran from the parking lot to the front gate. As he approached the gate, he saw his brother Jim getting close to the front gate. John gave it one last push and ran with everything he had left in him. He got up to his brother and shoved him out of the way. John did it! He was the first in line. Jim, his brother, was behind him in line.

The ticket gate attendee opened the gate and John held out his ticket proudly, saying loudly, "I am the 1,000,000th ticket holder." The barcode on the ticket was scanned and nothing happened. John just stood there looking befuddled. The ticket gate attendee asked him to move to the side, so the next fan could enter the stadium.

Jim held out his ticket and as soon as it was scanned, lights and sirens went off because he was the 1,000,000th fan. Jim was escorted to the owner's box, where he enjoyed the game.

John got angry about losing his brother and demanded an answer about the fan count. The previous game's attendance was reported incorrectly, under by one. Therefore, it was not the first fan through the gate but the second who would be the 1,000,000th fan.

John stayed for the game, after all, he was a team fan. After the game, he returned to his car to find he had three gifts on the windshield. The gifts were three tickets, one for running a red light, one for an illegal left turn, and one for parking in an accessible parking space. He thought if he had been like his brother Jim and not tried to control the event, he might have won a much better prize.

Commentary:

When we read about first verses second-born children in the Bible, it is clear God favors the second born, especially in Genesis. Why? Because it is the second born who follows God more than the firstborn. Starting with Cain and Abel, it is Abel who is favored because he brought a better sacrifice to the Lord. It is the second born of Abraham, Isaac, who received the covenant God made with Abraham. Jacob was the second-born son of Isaac and when Joseph asked Jacob to bless his sons, it is Jacob who gives the higher blessing to the second son.

Solomon inherited the throne from David. Solomon was the second son of David and Bathsheba. So, the first is not always the first. Being born first does not automatically place you at the front of the line. In the Kingdom of heaven, your place in line is determined by what you do for God.

The Parable of the Hidden Treasure (Matthew 13:44)

The Parable:

44 "The kingdom of heaven is like treasure hidden in a field. When a man found it, he hid it again, and then in his joy went and sold all he had and bought that field. (Mat 13:44 NIV)

The Modern Parable:

A young man grew up in a non-religious home, which is very common in the late 20th and 21st centuries. Eventually, he graduated from college, got married and had a family. When he reached his mid-30's he wondered if there was more to the world than what he was currently doing. As numerous people do when they reach the age of 35, they contemplate the future and the possibilities. This young man turned to the major religions of the world seeking an answer to the why are we here question and what is it we are expected to be doing. He always believed in God but did not call upon Him too often, just for the big questions.

During his search, he came upon a treasure. It was the answer for which he was searching. Finding the treasure filled him with joy, but he knew he did not know enough about the treasure to value it as he should. So instead of sharing the treasure with others, he buried it deep within his heart until he understood the true meaning and purpose of the treasure.

He knew other people who had discovered the treasure, but by their behavior and actions, it was clear they did not understand the value of the treasure they possessed. This was confusing to the young man. How can one discover this wonderful treasure and then ignore the fact they possessed the treasure? This was extremely confusing to the young man.

His solution was to learn everything he could about the treasure. When he understood the power and beauty of the treasure, he could then show the world that he too, like numerous others not only discovered the treasure but lived by what he learned from the treasure.

The only way to learn about the treasure was attending a learning institute which only taught about the treasure. But it costs a lot of money to attend. So, the young man attended the institute because he determined discovering the purpose of the treasure was far more important than worldly things. So, he sold many of his worldly possessions to pay for the classes. The young man's heart was filled with joy as he learned about the treasure he had found.

One day he completed the first steps of his learnings, and he showed the world what he found the treasure and understood its value. He walked the walk and talked the talk. He also continued to learn about the treasure.

Commentary:

There appears in many cases to be a difference between persons who are raised from childhood in the church and those who come to know Jesus as adults. Perhaps it is because the adults want to know Jesus. There are also persons who are raised in the church, revolt by leaving the church, then return in later life rediscovering the treasure God gave them. In this modern parable the young man grew up without a religious background. He graduated from college, got married, has a family and the good things in life. But his life was empty.

To fill the emptiness, he searched for the meaning and purpose of life. His search took him to the religions of the world. In so doing he discovered the greatest treasure one can find!

Jesus Christ. The young man realized the treasure he had discovered but also understood the need to learn about Jesus as God's Son and what it means to have Jesus as Lord and Savior.

Therefore, he buried his treasure, Jesus, deep into his heart. Unfortunately, his experience with church goers was not positive. So, many churchgoers did not practice the ways of Jesus even when they were in the church building, he started visiting. The young man was so determined to learn about Jesus, he let go of the negativity many church goers were showing and to learn what the right way to show the treasure was. The church he attended could not do this, so he enrolled in seminary.

Seminary was expensive, so he had to sell a lot of his worldly possessions to pay the tuition. But it was worth every penny to learn about Jesus. Now equipped with the understanding of Jesus, he showed the world the treasure he found, buried, and now uncovered because he knew the true value of Jesus.

The Parable of the Luncheon (Luke 14:12-15)

The Parable:

[12] Then Jesus said to his host, "When you give a luncheon or dinner, do not invite your friends, your brothers or sisters, your relatives, or your rich neighbors; if you do, they may invite you back and so you will be repaid. [13] But when you give a banquet, invite the poor, the crippled, the lame, the blind, [14] and you will be blessed. Although they cannot repay you, you will be repaid at the resurrection of the righteous." [15] When one of those at the table with him heard this, he said to Jesus, "Blessed is the one who will eat at the feast in the kingdom of God." (Luk 14:12-15 NIV)

The Modern Parable:

There was a church on the edge of a city. The people of the church lived in the suburbs and would travel to the church. The church decided to hold dinner once a week with a time of worship. The dinner was well attended and was considered a success. The church had installed an LED advertising panel in front of the church so that the public could learn about the various worship celebrations and church activities. The church's computer expert developed a nice program which would read the church's Google calendar and would display the events on the LED advertising panel (sign board). What a nice idea the church leadership thought. No more manual programming of the panel. It would always be up to date!

Of course, the weekly dinner and worship was an event on the Google calendar, and it appeared on the advertising panel. After two weeks of advertising, several city people started attending the dinner and worship. The church people who attended the dinner were surprised initially, but they welcomed the city people. The weekly dinner worship event became an outreach event for the church. The city people who attended were low income or on welfare. The church people found it a joy to share Christ with these people. After all, Jesus said, "go out and make disciples."

Word spread throughout the church about the change that occurred with the weekly dinner and worship. What surprised the church attendees of the dinner was the loud noise from several church members who did not attend the dinner, that poor city people were allowed into the church. They felt their church was an upper middle class only church. They felt they were superior to the poor city people. These people got so angry they did everything they could to stop the dinner.

The sad part of the story is the church leadership agreed to the demands of the people who wanted the dinner and worship to stop and they stopped the event.

Commentary:

The initial intent of the dinner/worship was for the people of the church. The event changed from a banquet for the elite into a banquet for the poor. The people who started the event became the servants who brought the food and served the poor. Jesus tells us we should help those in need with no demand of something in return. When we share our blessings with the poor, we are sharing the love of God with all people.

The Parable of the Mustard Seed (Mark 4:30-34)

The Parable:

[30] Again he said, "What shall we say the kingdom of God is like, or what parable shall we use to describe it? [31] It is like a mustard seed, which is the smallest of all seeds on earth. [32] Yet when planted, it grows and becomes the largest of all garden plants, with such big branches that the birds can perch in its shade." [33] With many similar parables Jesus spoke the word to them, as much as they could understand. [34] He did not say anything to them without using a parable. But when he was alone with his own disciples, he explained everything. (Mk. 4:30-34 NIV)

The Modern Parable:

I love watching young children under the age of six years old. They have a natural curiosity to discover everything around them. They know they are protected by their loving parents. They do not worry about if there will be a next meal or not. They have complete faith and trust in their parents. The children can play under the protection of their parents, who form an umbrella above the children. All the needs of the children are supplied without question with unconditional love for them.

Commentary:

This parable can also be found in the Gospel of Matthew 13:31-32. What is fascinating about the Scripture is you can see different messages in it depending on how you read it.

IN the book of Daniel: [10] These are the visions I saw while lying in bed: I looked, and there before me stood a tree in the middle of the land. Its height was enormous. [11] The tree grew large and strong and its top touched the sky; it was visible to the ends of the earth. [12] Its leaves were beautiful, its fruit abundant, and on it was food for all. Under it the wild animals found shelter, and the birds lived in its branches; from it every creature was fed. (Dan. 4:10-12 NIV)

This examination of the parable uses the imagery of a tree. The mustard seed grows to be the largest garden plant and a mustard seed can also grow into being a tree. So, continuing with the idea of a tree in Daniel's vision:

1. It was in the center of the earth.
2. Height was great, or large.
3. The tree was strong.
4. It reached to the end of all the earth. So, it covered the earth.
5. Much fruit was upon the tree. It was abounding in food.
6. There was meat/food for all. So, it fed all for all flesh was fed of it.
7. The beasts of the field dwelt under it and the fowl of the air dwelt in it.[5]

We can also investigate Genesis and discover:

[9] The LORD God made all kinds of trees grow out of the ground-- trees that were pleasing to the eye and good for food. In the middle of the garden were the tree of life and the tree of the knowledge of good and evil. (Gen. 2:9 NIV)

In Genesis we read about the tree in the middle of the garden which was the tree of life.

---

[5] "Daniel Bible Prophecy." Daniel Bible Prophecy - Daniel 4. Accessed November 16, 2017. http://www.danielbibleprophecy.org/daniel4.html.

The tree in Daniel's vision gave life because of the fruit that it produced.

> [29] Then God said, "I give you every seed-bearing plant on the face of the whole earth and every tree that has fruit with seed in it. They will be yours for food. (Gen. 1:29 NIV)

God gave us every fruit bearing tree as food except for one in the Garden of Eden. We are not living in the Garden of Eden, so all the fruits produced by trees can be eaten freely. The fruit of these trees will sustain our lives.

The Daniel tree imagery tells us that the branches of the tree will be large and strong enough to support any birds that wish to perch on it. The tree in this case covers the Earth, which would symbolize God's love and grace for us, which covers the Earth. Jesus' parable is not about covering the entire Earth but covers a garden which can be symbolic of the Earth. The imagery of Eden comes into play because in Genesis the Garden is the entire earth to Adam and Eve. The Tree of Life is a symbol of life which comes from God (which sat in the middle of the Garden with the Tree of the knowledge of good and evil). Without a doubt, it is the largest tree on the Earth.

The tree supports the birds and other animals, offers us food, also offers us shade from the heat of the day. The Kingdom of God is like a large, strong tree because God protects us from the evil of Satan by shading us from his influence. Like the tree, God provides our daily bread – the physical food and the spiritual food we need to live.

The large tree in the garden needs nothing from us to grow and prosper. Analogously, God requires nothing from us. His love for us comes with no strings attached. To honor God, those who accept his shading of love and grace will want to follow His Law so, that all people can live in harmony under the Lord.

One more point about the Tree in the Garden is that there is God's peace under the Tree. If animals can be brought together under the Tree and they are going to eat the fruit of the tree rather than each other than God's Shalom has been established. The Kingdom of God will have the Great Shalom restored.

The Parable of the Prodigal Son (Luke 15:11-32)

The Parable:

11 Jesus continued: "There was a man who had two sons. 12 The younger one said to his
father, 'Father, give me my share of the estate.' So he divided his property between them. 13
"Not long after that, the younger son got together all he had, set off for a distant country
and there squandered his wealth in wild living. 14 After he had spent everything, there was a
severe famine in that whole country, and he began to be in need. 15 So he went and hired
himself out to a citizen of that country, who sent him to his fields to feed pigs. 16 He
longed to fill his stomach with the pods that the pigs were eating, but no one gave him
anything. 17 "When he came to his senses, he said, 'How many of my father's hired servants
have food to spare, and here I am starving to death! 18 I will set out and go back to my
father and say to him: Father, I have sinned against heaven and against you. 19 I am no
longer worthy to be called your son; make me like one of your hired servants.' 20 So he got
up and went to his father. "But while he was still a long way off, his father saw him and
was filled with compassion for him; he ran to his son, threw his arms around him and
kissed him. 21 "The son said to him, 'Father, I have sinned against heaven and against you. I
am no longer worthy to be called your son.' 22 "But the father said to his servants, 'Quick!
Bring the best robe and put it on him. Put a ring on his finger and sandals on his feet. 23
Bring the fattened calf and kill it. Let's have a feast and celebrate. 24 For this son of mine
was dead and is alive again; he was lost and is found.' So, they began to celebrate. 25
"Meanwhile, the older son was in the field. When he came near the house, he heard music
and dancing. 26 So he called one of the servants and asked him what was going on. 27 'Your
brother has come,' he replied, 'and your father has killed the fattened calf because he has
him back safe and sound.' 28 "The older brother became angry and refused to go in. So, his

father went out and pleaded with him. 29 But he answered his father, 'Look! All these years
I've been slaving for you and never disobeyed your orders. Yet you never gave me even a
young goat so I could celebrate with my friends. 30 But when this son of yours who has
squandered your property with prostitutes comes home, you kill the fattened calf for him!'
31 "'My son,' the father said, 'you are always with me, and everything I have is yours. 32 But
we had to celebrate and be glad, because this brother of yours was dead and is alive again;
he was lost and is found.'" (Luk 15:11-32 NIV)

The Modern Parable:

My son turned 18 years old this past summer. He graduated with honors from High School and was going to attend one of those fancy ivy league colleges. Unfortunately, the college was far away, and I knew I would miss our Sunday morning chats. I always hoped that while at college, he would find time for me. The Ivy League College was expensive, and I wanted to help him pay for college, so I took on a second job on the weekends.

During his four years at college, I did not see him very much. When he came home, he was more interested in borrowing the car keys than he was sitting down and chatting with me like we did before college. I thought I lost him to the glamor he found in the world.

After some time being on his own after college, he matured to discover the glamor of the world did not fill his soul. He did not have any kind of spiritual life. For him, life became a game of work and play, but it had no meaning or purpose. After discovering this, my son came home. He wanted to return to our weekly chats. He felt when he was at home, he had a sense of belonging and acceptance. At home, he was accepted for who he was while in the world's glamor he was constantly judged. He felt anguished over the error of his way, so he sought a therapist. The therapist told him he should return home because he would be forgiven for his errors, and he could correct his life. So, he went home.

Upon his return, I had a party with the entire family to announce my joy at my son's return. Some of my relatives did not understand why I would hold a party for my son's return. After all, they said he dishonored me by leaving and ignoring me for so many years. I would not let them tear down my joy, for my son had returned to me. Our Sunday chats would start up again. The joy of having my son returning to me melted the years he was away from me from my memory. My son never again thought about what he could have outside the family. Instead, he cherished his time with family. Our weekly chats returned!

Commentary:

Anyone who has ever read and tried to understand Jesus' parable is aware they can have multiple meanings. In this rendition of the parable, the son is anyone who strays from God. This often happens with teenagers who reach maturity and can make their own decisions. When young, they enjoyed Sunday School and learning about the biblical stories. While in High School and/or College, they decide it is not "cool" to be religious. Usually, peer pressure enters the picture. Then in time, they get married and have kids and decide God is important. Numerous times, they wished they never walked out on God. But God takes them back into the family without question. God's grace is to all. Even those who walk out on God.

The Parable of the Seed and Sickle (Mark 4:26-29)

The Parable:

26 He also said, "This is what the kingdom of God is like. A man scatters seed on the
ground. 27 Night and day, whether he sleeps or gets up, the seed sprouts and grows, though
he does not know how. 28 All by itself the soil produces grain-- first the stalk, then the
head, then the full kernel in the head. 29 As soon as the grain is ripe, he puts the sickle to it,
because the harvest has come. (Mk. 4:26-29 NIV)

The Modern Parable:

There was a husband and wife who had four children. They had a beautiful house custom-built to give each child a bedroom with a connected bathroom. They showered the children with everything they needed and wanted. They treated the children the same, showering them with their love. The parents attended every choir concert, little league baseball game, and any event each child was a part. They took the children on lavish vacations and gave them numerous gifts during the year, especially at Christmas and birthdays. Three of the children grew up, went to college, and became quite successful. The fourth child rebelled during high school, barely graduating, and moves between minimum wage jobs and is lost in determining what to do in life. So, what went wrong?

Commentary:

In Jesus' day, and before, the harvest of grain was done by hand. The parable draws one's attention to the fact that a sickle was used for the harvest. The imagery of the sickle is critical to the understanding of the parable. The cultural aspect of hands verses sickles can be seen in:

> [25] If you enter your neighbor's grainfield, you may pick kernels with your hands, but you must not put a sickle to their standing grain. (Deut. 23:25 NIV)

So, the use of the sickle is for the owner of the field only and we know in the day's culture the sickle was rarely used for harvesting. Since this is a kingdom parable then it is God who is the owner of the field. As the owner of the field, God planted the grain. Since we have free will and can make our own choices, God's people can develop a true love and faith in our God, or we cannot. The determination of our life to be good, or evil, is something each of us will determine. Surely, we can pray for wisdom and guidance, and we will receive it but ultimately, we make the determination how to live. Therefore, the parable saying, "he does not know" tells us God does not exercise his extreme power over used to determine our future.

The man sowing seeds does not influence the growth of the grain. It can be assumed the soil was prepared with the nutrients and irrigation. Then the seed grows as it will.

The imagery of the sickle takes us to Jeremiah.

> [6] Cut off from Babylon the sower, and the reaper with his sickle at harvest. Because of the sword of the oppressor let everyone return to their own people, let everyone flee to their own land. [17] "Israel is a scattered flock that lions have chased away. The first to devour them was the king of Assyria; the last to crush their bones was Nebuchadnezzar king of Babylon." [18] Therefore this is what the LORD Almighty, the God of Israel, says: "I will punish the king of Babylon and his land as I punished the king of Assyria. (Jer. 50:16-18 NIV)

> [13] Swing the sickle, for the harvest is ripe. Come, trample the grapes, for the winepress is

full and the vats overflow-- so great is their wickedness!" [14] Multitudes, multitudes in the valley of decision! For the day of the LORD is near in the valley of decision. (Joel 3:13-14 NIV)

In both Jeremiah and Joel, the sickle is used as a symbol of God judging the harvest. The Kingdom of God will be a time of judgment. For those who grew up well and followed the ways of the Torah and the commandments will be judged well in God's sight. Also, those who followed the ways of Jesus and spent their energy to become like the Master will be saved. The sickle will harvest everyone. However, the imagery from Jeremiah and Joel speaks about the judgment against those who are evil or wicked. Justice will come to them.

At the time of the Kingdom of God, the innocent and true to God will also be judged. The people who are good in the sight of the Lord will be granted homage in Heaven while the others will be condemned to Hell.

NIV **Isaiah 5:1** I will sing for the one I love a song about his vineyard: My loved one had a vineyard on a fertile hillside. [2] He dug it up and cleared it of stones and planted it with the choicest vines. He built a watchtower in it and cut out a winepress as well. Then he looked for a crop of good grapes, but it yielded only bad fruit. [3] "Now you dwellers in Jerusalem and people of Judah, judge between me and my vineyard. [4] What more could have been done for my vineyard than I have done for it? When I looked for good grapes, why did it yield only bad? [5] Now I will tell you what I am going to do to my vineyard: I will take away its hedge, and it will be destroyed; I will break down its wall, and it will be trampled. [6] I will make it a wasteland, neither pruned nor cultivated, and briers and thorns will grow there. I will command the clouds not to rain on it." [7] The vineyard of the LORD Almighty is the nation of Israel, and the people of Judah are the vines he

> delighted in. And he looked for justice, but saw bloodshed; for righteousness, but heard cries of dis (Isa. 5:1-7 NIV)

This Hebraic parable supports Jesus' parable. In this parable we learn God sets up the perfect garden for growth. However, God is telling us through Isaiah that even though only good grapes were planted some of the grapes grew up as bad grapes. Free will is demonstrated here. God gives us the best then each of us decides whether to follow the laws and precepts of God or not. How much more can God supply to us? The fertile land, the rain, even taking care of it yet the briers and thorns grow.

Jesus' parable he says the Sower of the seed decides to leave the field alone. But when the harvest comes the first thing the harvester does is to take the sickle to it. Why? Because the thorns and thistles grew and required a sickle to cut them down. Then the harvester will have to spend the time to separate the good from the bad.

On the Day of Judgment God will separate the good from the evil, the wheat from the chaff.

The Parable of the Talents (Matthew 25:14-30)

The Parable:

14 "Again, it will be like a man going on a journey, who called his servants and entrusted his wealth to them. 15 To one he gave five bags of gold, to another two bags, and to another one bag, each according to his ability. Then he went on his journey. 16 The man who had received five bags of gold went at once and put his money to work and gained five bags more. 17 So also, the one with two bags of gold gained two more. 18 But the man who had received one bag went off, dug a hole in the ground and hid his master's money. 19 "After a long time the master of those servants returned and settled accounts with them. 20 The man who had received five bags of gold brought the other five. 'Master,' he said, 'you entrusted me with five bags of gold. See, I have gained five more.' 21 "His master replied, 'Well done, good and faithful servant! You have been faithful with a few things; I will put you in charge of many things. Come and share your master's happiness!' 22 "The man with two bags of gold also came. 'Master,' he said, 'you entrusted me with two bags of gold; see, I have gained two more.' 23 "His master replied, 'Well done, good and faithful servant! You have been faithful with a few things; I will put you in charge of many things. Come and share your master's happiness!' 24 "Then the man who had received one bag of gold came. 'Master,' he said, 'I knew that you are a hard man, harvesting where you have not sown and gathering where you have not scattered seed. 25 So I was afraid and went out and hid your gold in the ground. See, here is what belongs to you.' 26 "His master replied, 'You wicked, lazy servant! So you knew that I harvest where I have not sown and gather where I have not scattered seed? 27 Well then, you should have put my money on deposit with the bankers, so that when I returned I would have received it back with interest. 28 "'So take the bag of gold from him and give it to the one who has ten bags. 29 For whoever has will be given more, and they will have an abundance. Whoever does not have, even what they have

will be taken from them. [30] And throw that worthless servant outside, into the darkness, where there will be weeping and gnashing of teeth." (Mat 25:14-30 NIV)

The Modern Parable:

This is the tale of two churches which were of the same denomination. One was on the north end of the city, while the other was on the south end. The north end church was in a nice neighborhood of mainly middle-class neighbors. The south end church was in a dangerous neighborhood of neighbors who were on welfare and government help. The people in both churches knew Jesus was for everyone, but each did it uniquely.

The south end church opened the doors to their sanctuary 24 hours a day. They removed the materials in the sanctuary which had value, the hymnals, and other items. In place of the hymnals, they created small songbooks, so any visitors could sing a hymn. They also created a booklet of prayers for the visitors to use. On cold nights, they had hot coffee available and every night there were sandwiches available. Several homeless people from the area would come into the church sanctuary to get a good night's sleep, especially in the cold months or when it was raining outside.

The north end church keeps the doors locked always except on Sunday morning. On Sundays they had security guards at the doors to ensure only members were allowed into the church. This church did not do anything for the community. Their mission and outreach programs consisted of giving money to a city charity organization and food bank.

One Sunday the pastor of the south end church came to church and discovered some vandalism in the sanctuary. At first the pastor was angry. He encouraged his church members to open their doors in charity and look at what happened. Then he thought about it and decided that opening the church to the poor and needy was what Jesus would want them to do. After all the church had tripled its attendance over the past 5 years since it opened its doors. Many of the homeless people stayed on Sunday morning to partake in the worship celebration. The church members could help several homeless people to get back on their feet. The south end church was making disciples.

During the same five-year period, the north end church membership and Sunday worship attendance had diminished in half. They did not have any members from the neighborhood. The community did not know what the church was all about. The church became irrelevant.

One day, the Bishop of the denomination paid a visit to the city. He wanted to meet with both churches. At the south end church, he praised them, telling them that Jesus had given them resources and would be so pleased that they took the risk and made disciples. At the north end church, he talked with them about how much longer their church would remain open. It could no longer subsidize itself, and the denomination would not send any more money to support them.

While the south end church members risked it all, they celebrated that day while the north end church was weeping and gnashing their teeth.

Commentary:

The servants in Jesus' parable were risk takers for the enlargement of the kingdom. In the modern parable, the church that took the risk of making disciples and did not allow the set back of vandalism stop them from making disciples. That church became relevant to the community in which it lived. The church became a place where the neediest could find Christ's love and grace. There was a church which held a community dinner in a poorer neighborhood. At each dinner, someone who attended kept stealing a roll of toilet paper. The sexton became concerned about this situation. Not that a roll of toilet paper was being stolen, but some congregation members might hear of it and shut down the outreach program.

If you want your church to flourish; you have to do the ministry of Jesus Christ no matter what the risk. A church that does not do the ministry of Jesus will die because Jesus will no longer give the church the resources it needs. A good example of this can be found in Revelation chapter two.

The Parable of the Vine and the Branch (John 15:1-8)

The parable:

NIV **John 15:1** "I am the true vine, and my Father is the gardener. 2 He cuts off every branch in me that bears no fruit, while every branch that does bear fruit he prunes so that it will be even more fruitful. 3 You are already clean because of the word I have spoken to you. 4 Remain in me, as I also remain in you. No branch can bear fruit by itself; it must remain in the vine. Neither can you bear fruit unless you remain in me. 5 "I am the vine; you are the branches. If you remain in me and I in you, you will bear much fruit; apart from me you can do nothing. 6 If you do not remain in me, you are like a branch that is thrown away and withers; such branches are picked up, thrown into the fire and burned. 7 If you remain in me and my words remain in you, ask whatever you wish, and it will be done for you. 8 This is to my Father's glory, that you bear much fruit, showing yourselves to be my disciples. (Joh 15:1-8 NIV)

The Modern Parable:

When I was a teenager in high school, I learned how to play the great game of chess. I studied the game at 13 and I joined the United States Chess Federation. At my first tournament, I achieved a class "A" rating for my performance. I loved the game so much that I studied the games played by the great masters and spent hours trying to improve my skills. Becoming connected to the United States Chess Federation opened a door which allowed me access to chess books, equipment and persons who could help me learn the game.

Then I went to college and my attention turned away from chess and to other things. I let my United States Chess Federation membership expire. I did not study the game or play very much. For the next 30 years I did not think much about the game.

Then a new friend told me that he was a chess player, and he reintroduced me to the game which I loved so much as a teenager. I reconnected with the United States Chess Federation by renewing my membership. I started to play in rated chess tournaments. I began to study the games of the great masters and worked on improving my skills. It was not long after this that I entered my first rated tournament and was able to achieve my rating from when I was a teenager.

Reconnecting with the United States Chess Federation opened the door to access to all kinds of information about chess, equipment, and access to people that could help me better my game. So, today I am active in the sport of chess, and I now help kids learn about chess because I found it and run a scholastic chess club.

Commentary:

A lesson from the story is that each of us handles our own actions and our decisions. It was my decision to disconnect from the United States Chess Federation and to stop playing the game. It was also my decision to reconnect with the Federation and start playing the game again. Each of us must decide in our lives that will affect our future. It is the same way as our relationship with God. We connect ourselves to our Lord Jesus Christ through baptism and it is up to us to decide whether we are going to be a branch on his vine that will produce fruit, or will we allow ourselves to wither away?

If we stay connected to Jesus, the vine, then we will receive all the spiritual nutrition that we need to keep ourselves alive in Christ. Producing fruit for Jesus can be done. Preaching the Gospel is the most potent way. Remember that preaching the Gospel does not mean using only words. Whenever we do acts of kindness and love in the name of Jesus, we are preaching his Gospel and showing the world how much God loves us through his son Jesus.

If we stop accepting the spiritual powers from the vine, that is from Jesus, by not preaching the Gospel, by not attending worship, by not tithing, and by not acting as a part of the family of God then eventually we will wither away spiritually, and we will be disconnected from the vine. John Wesley, the founder of Methodism, called this backsliding. He also noted that it is possible for us to backslide so much that we will lose our salvation. In order not to lose your salvation, you must decide of whether or not to follow through and preach the Gospel. The church exists to refuel our energies each week and to remind us of the distress before us from Satan, so that we continue to be a fruitful branch on the vine. Being fruitful is being spiritually alive!

The Parable of the Wicked Tenants (Mark 12:1-12)

The Parable:

[NIV] Jesus then began to speak to them in parables: "A man planted a vineyard. He put a wall around it, dug a pit for the winepress and built a watchtower. Then he rented the vineyard to some farmers and moved to another place. [2] At harvest time he sent a servant to the tenants to collect from them some of the fruit of the vineyard. [3] But they seized him, beat him and sent him away empty-handed. [4] Then he sent another servant to them; they struck this man on the head and treated him shamefully. [5] He sent still another, and that one they killed. He sent many others; some of them they beat, others they killed. [6] "He had one left to send, a son, whom he loved. He sent him last of all, saying, 'They will respect my son.' [7] "But the tenants said to one another, 'This is the heir. Come, let's kill him, and the inheritance will be ours.' [8] So they took him and killed him, and threw him out of the vineyard. [9] "What then will the owner of the vineyard do? He will come and kill those tenants and give the vineyard to others. [10] Haven't you read this passage of Scripture: "'The stone the builders rejected has become the cornerstone; [11] the Lord has done this, and it is marvelous in our eyes'?" [12] Then the chief priests, the teachers of the law and the elders looked for a way to arrest him because they knew he had spoken the parable against them. But they were afraid of the crowd; so they left him and went away. (Mk. 12:1-12 NIV)

The Modern Parable:

Do you remember the days of vinyl records that were used for music? You need a special device called a record player to listen to music. There was an audiophile who loved to hear music on those old records. Was he an audiophile because he did not have a problem listening to the records with the noise and skips that were a part of the recording? But this man loved his music. One day, his children purchased a new CD player for him as a birthday present. Along with the CD player, they purchased all of his music in CD form. Now the audiophile could listen to the pure music without the scratches and skips.

You would think that this was a wonderful gift. However, the audiophile got angry with his children. He could not accept that his music could be on any media than scratchy vinyl records. He destroyed the CD player and CD recordings.

When his children asked him why he did this, he responded that he just did not want change. He believed that change was bad. Even though the music was still the music, the church to a CD player was just wrong. He rejected a new way of thinking.

Commentary:

Jesus could have based his parable on the story of the Joseph story. Here is why.

> [16] He replied, "I'm looking for my brothers. Can you tell me where they are grazing their
> flocks?" [17] "They have moved on from here," the man answered. "I heard them say, 'Let's
> go to Dothan. '" So Joseph went after his brothers and found them near Dothan. [18] But
> they saw him in the distance, and before he reached them, they plotted to kill him. [19]
> "Here comes that dreamer!" they said to each other. [20] "Come now, let's kill him and
> throw him into one of these cisterns and say that a ferocious animal devoured him. Then we'll see what comes of his dreams." (Genesis 37:16-20)

A point about the Joseph story must be made before continuing.

> [21] When Reuben heard this, he tried to rescue him from their hands. "Let's not take his life," he said. (Gen. 37:16-21 NIV)

> [25] As they sat down to eat their meal, they looked up and saw a caravan of Ishmaelites
> coming from Gilead. Their camels were loaded with spices, balm and myrrh, and they
> were on their way to take them down to Egypt. [26] Judah said to his brothers, "What will
> we gain if we kill our brother and cover up his blood? [27] Come, let's sell him to the
> Ishmaelites and not lay our hands on him; after all, he is our brother, our own flesh and
> blood." His brothers agreed. (Gen. 37:25-27 NIV)

> [31] Then they got Joseph's robe, slaughtered a goat and dipped the robe in the blood. [32]
> They took the ornate robe back to their father and said, "We found this. Examine it to
> see whether it is your son's robe." [33] He recognized it and said, "It is my son's robe! Some
> ferocious animal has devoured him. Joseph has surely been torn to pieces." (Gen. 37:31-
> 33 NIV)

So far as Jacob thought and the way the brothers acted, Joseph was dead. So, the son who was sent to check on the brothers (the tenants of Jacob's land – metaphorically) was killed by them. Can the story be a foreshadowing of the death of God's Son and the Resurrection? From Jacob's point of view, his son Joseph was dead and then resurrected from the dead when he meets him in Egypt.

There would not have been nevertheless for the brothers to know what would happen to Joseph. During the Joseph story, he ends up in Egypt and becomes second in command to the Pharaoh of Egypt. There is a narrative story about Joseph's entry into Egypt and what happened to him before he became second in command.

A famine occurred in the land of Canaan and Jacob had to send his sons to Egypt to get grain. On the second trip to Egypt, Joseph revealed himself. Pharaoh tells Joseph to bring his whole family into Egypt and they settled in Goshen. Joseph becomes the cornerstone of the entire family. Without Joseph, his father Jacob and the entire family might have starved in Canaan or would have to sell themselves into slavery. So, Joseph saves the family and is the cornerstone of the survival of God's chosen people.

> [2] And God spoke to Israel in a vision at night and said, "Jacob! Jacob!" "Here I am," he replied. [3] "I am God, the God of your father," he said. "Do not be afraid to go down to Egypt, for I will make you into a great nation there. (Gen. 46:2-3 NIV)

Going back to the tenants on the land. Jacob bought a field and set up his tent.

> [18] After Jacob came from Paddan Aram, he arrived safely at the city of Shechem in Canaan and camped within sight of the city. [19] For a hundred pieces of silver, he bought from the sons of Hamor, the father of Shechem, the plot of ground where he pitched his tent. [20] There he set up an altar and called it El Elohe Israel. (Gen. 33:18-20 NIV)

Joseph was the favorite son of Jacob.

> [3] Now Israel loved Joseph more than any of his other sons, because he had been born to him in his old age; and he made an ornate robe for him. (Gen. 37:3 NIV)

Since Jacob sent Joseph out into the fields to find his brothers to bring a message to them, a logical conclusion is Joseph did not have to work the fields. So, the "tenants" of the field are the ten brothers (Benjamin was too young to be in the fields). So, Jacob sent his son, his favorite son, to the fields to talk with the tenants. The brothers wanted to kill Joseph and not for Reuben's intervention they would have. As stated earlier, the story the brothers gave their father was that Joseph was dead.

The parable of the wicked tenants could have been a parable based on the Joseph story.

Jesus becomes the cornerstone of the family of God in the same way Joseph was the cornerstone of the family of God's chosen.

The Pharisee and the Tax Collector (Luke 18:9-14)

The Parable:

9 To some who were confident of their own righteousness and looked down on everyone else, Jesus told this parable: 10 "Two men went up to the temple to pray, one a Pharisee and the other a tax collector. 11 The Pharisee stood by himself and prayed: 'God, I thank you that I am not like other people-- robbers, evildoers, adulterers-- or even like this tax collector. 12 I fast twice a week and give a tenth of all I get.' 13 "But the tax collector stood at a distance. He would not even look up to heaven, but beat his breast and said, 'God, have mercy on me, a sinner.' 14 "I tell you that this man, rather than the other, went home justified before God. For all those who exalt themselves will be humbled, and those who humble themselves will be exalted." (Lk. 18:9-14 NIV)

The Modern Parable:

There were two men who went to church on a particular Sunday. Both were dressed well and looked wealthy. One man was rich while the other was poor. The rich man gave $100/week to the offering and was proud of his $100. He looked at the poor man, not knowing that he was poor, who only put $10/week into the church offering. The rich man boasted about with $100/week. As it turns out, the $10/week that the poor man gave to the church was 10%, a tithing, of his income while the rich man's $100 week was less than 1% of his income. Which one is being true to God?

Commentary:

The Greek educational method teaches that the humble tax collector is the one Jesus determines will get into heaven because the Pharisee boasts about his being in alignment with the Laws of the Torah. A substantial number of books on the Parables will say the same thing.

Going to the Temple to pray the Pharisee offered prayers he was a good Jew by following the Laws of the Torah. This is an echo of the Hebrew Scriptures.[6] The Pharisee was doing exactly what the Law says.

> 13 Then say to the LORD your God: "I have removed from my house the sacred portion and have given it to the Levite, the foreigner, the fatherless and the widow, according to all you commanded. I have not turned aside from your commands nor have I forgotten any of them. 14 I have not eaten any of the sacred portion while I was in mourning, nor have I removed any of it while I was unclean, nor have I offered any of it to the dead. I have obeyed the LORD my God; I have done everything you commanded me. 15 Look down from heaven, your holy dwelling place, and bless your people Israel and the land you have given us as you promised on oath to our ancestors, a land flowing with milk and honey." 16 The LORD your God commands you this day to follow these decrees and laws; carefully observe them with all your heart and with all your soul. (Deut. 26:13-16 NIV)

You can read several verses before 26:13 and see the commands of what to do for the Lord before making the boast. Therefore, the Pharisee simply follows the Laws. Pharisees get a bad rap with Christians because the Greek interpretation always makes them look bad. In this case the Pharisee was doing what was right.

The tax collector was also doing the right thing. His prayer is an echo of Psalm 51.[7]

---

[6] "Interpreting the Parables," Craig Blomberg, pg. 343

[7] IBID, pg. 346

> [3] For I know my transgressions, and my sin is always before me. [4] Against you, you only, have I sinned and done what is evil in your sight; so you are right in your verdict and justified when you judge. (Ps. 51:3-4 NIV)

So, coming before the Lord in prayer to confess sin and to request forgiveness is also biblical. So, Jesus has placed two people each doing what the Scriptures call for against each other. What did Jesus's listeners hear? Jesus is giving us an extension to the Law. Following the Law is extremely important. However, admitting to one's sin and praying for God's salvation and forgiveness is also important. Admitting sin is a necessary component of our salvation.

Who can follow all the Laws of the Torah? Jesus would be the only one who could. Since the rest of us cannot follow all the Laws perfectly, we need to accept that we do sin and those who will admit to our sin will be the ones who will receive forgiveness and salvation.

So, for the listeners of Jesus, they received a new learning about the Scriptures. It is important to follow the Laws and come before God and confess sin and repent.

The Wedding Feast Parable (Matthew 22:2-14)

The Parable:

2 "The kingdom of heaven is like a king who prepared a wedding banquet for his son. 3 He
sent his servants to those who had been invited to the banquet to tell them to come, but
they refused to come. 4 "Then he sent some more servants and said, 'Tell those who have
been invited that I have prepared my dinner: My oxen and fattened cattle have been
butchered, and everything is ready. Come to the wedding banquet.' 5 "But they paid no
attention and went off-- one to his field, another to his business. 6 The rest seized his
servants, mistreated them and killed them. 7 The king was enraged. He sent his army and
destroyed those murderers and burned their city. 8 "Then he said to his servants, 'The
wedding banquet is ready, but those I invited did not deserve to come. 9 So go to the street
corners and invite to the banquet anyone you find.' 10 So the servants went out into the
streets and gathered all the people they could find, the bad as well as the good, and the
wedding hall was filled with guests. 11 "But when the king came in to see the guests, he
noticed a man there who was not wearing wedding clothes. 12 He asked, 'How did you get
in here without wedding clothes, friend?' The man was speechless. 13 "Then the king told
the attendants, 'Tie him hand and foot, and throw him outside, into the darkness, where
there will be weeping and gnashing of teeth.' 14 "For many are invited, but few are chosen."
(Mat 22:2-14 NIV)

The Modern Parable:

A young couple fell in love, and after dating for a time got married. Both were from poor families and the two had just graduated from college with a mountain of debt. The couple got together and wrote out a guest list for the wedding. Before long, they noted there were over 300 names on the list. When they pooled their resources together with the small amount of money, their parents could contribute, they did not have enough money for a 300-person wedding. What were they going to do?

The solution they decided upon was to invite all 300 people to the wedding ceremony, but only 100 to the reception. So, they got an invitation put together for the wedding ceremony and sent it out to the 300 guests. The invitation specifically said, "invitation to the wedding ceremony only." With the invitation was a reply card and, on the card, and it said, "Please show the gift you will be bringing." About 1 month later, they sent a second invitation to the 100 people.

The wedding day came, and the couple were married, with 300 guests in attendance for the ceremony. As the people left the ceremony, there was a lot of discuss who were invited to the reception. There were many who felt they should have been invited to the reception because of their importance. They never discovered that the decision was determined by the gift they brought.

Commentary:

"For many are invited, but few are chosen." This is the last sentence of the parable and the most troubling. What are we to make of it? Considering today's life of the church, is Jesus saying people who are attending church today will not be chosen into heaven? If so, what are the criteria? We must be careful because this line of thinking takes us down the path of work righteousness.

Let us go to Genesis, where we read the story of Cain and Abel. Why was Abel's sacrifice more acceptable to God? A Jewish legend tells us Abel brought the first fruits of his harvest, the best he had, to offer God. Cain had lunch before coming before the Lord and he brought the leftovers from his lunch. So, God looked favorably at Abel's sacrifice because he gave the best.

So, to not flow into the problem of works righteousness, we must definitively say it is not the value of the sacrifice or a works righteousness evaluation but a question of is the sacrifice of first fruits, the absolute best, to God. Many come before God to offer a sacrifice, but how many give their best as the sacrifice? If you are not bringing your best to sacrifice to God, then perhaps you should not bring any sacrifice. It is clear from the Cain and Abel story that Cain should have waited to bring his best, rather than the leftovers.

Sacrifices today could comprise time, attitude, and money. The money part is simple because it is defined biblically as a tithe. The first check of the bills should give back to the work of the Lord. The time sacrifice should be how much? If we use the tithe calculation, then it is 10% of your time, let us say awake time. For most people that is 16 hours a day, so 1 hour 40 minutes. This time for God can be composed of many personal and sacrificial tasks. So, attending church for 1 hour a week and saying that is the time I give God is probably not giving God your best. The worst is sitting in a worship celebration awaiting the hour to be up.

Attitude toward God is easy, but attitude toward persons God places in authority over us in the church can be difficult. When pastors change in churches, there are people who leave the church because of the change. If God is a part of the pastorate decision-making process, then what attitude is being displayed? This can be expanded to include bishops, cardinals and popes. So, part of our sacrifice is working with leadership that we may not favor. Also, learning to let go of any animosity.

Saint Paul said, "God loves a happy giver." Those who are chosen from the population will be those who give their best sacrifice to God in all aspects of life.

The Parable of the Wheat and the Weeds (Matthew 13:24-30)

The Parable:

24 Jesus told them another parable: "The kingdom of heaven is like a man who sowed good
seed in his field. 25 But while everyone was sleeping, his enemy came and sowed weeds
among the wheat, and went away. 26 When the wheat sprouted and formed heads, then the
weeds also appeared. 27 "The owner's servants came to him and said, 'Sir, did not you sow
good seed in your field? Where then did the weeds come from?' 28 "'An enemy did this,' he
replied. "The servants asked him, 'Do you want us to go and pull them up?' 29 "'No,' he
answered, 'because while you are pulling the weeds, you may uproot the wheat with them.
30 Let both grow together until the harvest. At that time I will tell the harvesters: First
collect the weeds and tie them in bundles to be burned; then gather the wheat and bring it
into my barn.'" (Mat 13:24-30 NIV)

Modern Parable:

A new pastor was appointed to a church. The congregation welcomed the new pastor, but as with every new pastor, the people were wondering what she was going to say and try to make the congregation do. It did not take long to hear sermons about making disciples for Jesus Christ. After all, making disciples is the mission of the church and for a church to grow, it needs new disciples. Initially, the congregation did not react to this preaching. They had heard this line of reasoning before, but the pastors of the past never acted upon it.

But this pastor was different. She organized the church to go out and make disciples. She started seeker worship services and canvased the community, inviting everyone to learn about Jesus Christ. After a couple of months, the efforts started working. The Gospel of

Jesus Christ was spreading around the neighborhood.

There was a small group of people in the church who fully supported the pastor, believing in the church's mission. However, there was a small group of people who were completely against bringing any new people into the church. Most of the people of the church did not take notice and did not care about the feud that begun. All the services and programs that the church had been doing for years remained in place and these new disciples making activities were added to the church's schedule.

The pastor could maintain a negotiated balance between the establishment church and the new church that was emerging. The people who wanted to maintain the church were appeased, and the people who wanted to fulfill Christ's mission were also appeased. There was always some contention, but both prevailed.

Then one day a leader of the church asked did not Jesus say to make disciples and to educate them in the ways of the faith. "Yes, Jesus said that," replied the pastor. So, she was asked if, by holding onto the programs and services of the past, was the church fulfilling the second part of the mission? "Yes, it is," replied the pastor. Then the leader noted that the church was fulfilling the full mission of the church and not just a part of it.

Commentary:

Church is composed of three types of persons (generalizing here): (1) those who want to maintain the status quo at all costs; (2) those who want to be disciples of Jesus Christ; (3) those who come to church 1 hour a week to "fulfill their obligation." I'd first like to discuss the third type of person. They come to church because they have learned, probably from childhood, that they are required to do so. Then God will have favor on them and upon death they will go to heaven.

There will always be a group of people in the church who not only want the status quo, but will fight anyone trying to change it. In a world which is constantly changing, having a part of their lives that they can count on being the same week after week is important. Since churches rarely change and if they do, it is slower than a snail crawling, this is a great institution to belong to if you need a part of your life that is not changing.

Those who come to church once a week want nothing to do with the politics of the church. If their current worship service exists, and they are left alone, they are happy. The disciples of Jesus Christ in the church know they must fulfill the mission of the church. However, during the past almost 20 years, the mission has been refined to "making disciples for Jesus Christ." What happened to the second part of the Great Commission?

Whenever change is implemented in church for the following of Jesus' the mission, it is important to ensure that the current programming and schedule of the church are maintained. Everything necessary for disciple making needs to be added to the church's programming. But it caused problems with the status quo people (i.e. they feared the new people). Trying to convince the status quo people that the church needs to do both have difficulties to prevail.

The bottom line is in the church you need all three types! That sounds wrong, but for the church institution to survive, you need all three. Why? Because the biblical concept of tithing does not exist in many hearts. At least 90% of the people in the pews give to the church because they are attending a worship service and, in their minds, paying for that service. With that attitude it becomes clear why change is difficult. But we need these people because for the church to exist in the world today we need the money. That's sounds horrible and unbiblical, but it is a reality.

So, the formula for success is how to appease the three groups and grow the church by making disciples. A startup church will be successful if it decides up front which type of membership it wants. For survival it needs to be a disciple church and not a membership church. Disciples are obligated to Jesus Christ while members are obligated to the church as an institution. In some of the larger startup churches, members, not disciples, will start attending. If the leadership is not careful the membership will outnumber the discipleship.

In the parable, the discipleship persons are the wheat while the membership are the weeds in this parable. The two are hard to distinguish unless you are looking inside their offering envelopes. Jesus is telling us for the survival of the church we unfortunately need both. This can be seen in the Great Commission. At the time of judgment God will separate the members from the disciples.

www.ingramcontent.com/pod-product-compliance
Lightning Source LLC
LaVergne TN
LVHW082249150826
845677LV00009B/1584
9798230315483